I0463041

Time Management for Busy Executives

by

Lawrence G Fine

Time management for Busy Executives
Copyright © 2009 by (Kick It, LLC)

Table of Contents

Introduction

"No one has enough time, but everyone has all there is."

It has been said that once your start working, you no longer have control over your time. Project deadlines, client presentations and endless meetings seems to take up most of your day, sometimes even your nights. This leaves you with less time to spend with your family, friends and even time to spend for yourself.

People frequently have problems with time management for a wide variety of issues. In some cases it is simply because they are unaware that there are techniques out there that can help them to better utilize their time. Other individuals admittedly do not have the drive to implement any planning system into their lives or enjoy the 'rush' of working under pressure and meeting tight deadlines.

Unfortunately, the problem with this style of 'time management' is that it leads to stress, failed projects, missed opportunities and ultimately a lower sense of self-worth as well as complications regarding health issues.

Despite the many issues surrounding poor time management, many executives fail to take the time to implement a time management and scheduling program into their own lives because they fail to see the advantages of such a program. The most common excuse for failure to plan is simply that it takes too much time to do so. Irony aside, there are numerous advantages to time management and it is extremely important to consistently set aside time to take care of this important task.

While it does require time to set up and continually maintain a time management program, the most important advantage of doing so is that you will immediately gain time. A time management program will also help to motivate and inspire you as you begin to initiate your goals. Failure to plan often leads to procrastination and ultimately stress; implementing a time management program in your life will help to reduce avoidance, eliminate last minute cramming and reduce stress and anxiety.

In the following pages, we will present some of best known tips to help you get a handle on your schedule and begin efficiently managing your time to make the most of each and every day. no matter what emergencies you face.

Chapter 1 Managing your Time

One of the most important things to understand in learning how to efficiently manage your time is that there are several key components to handling any scheduling activities. Self knowledge and goals rank at the top of this list. In order for you to begin managing your time efficiently, you must first be aware of what is most important to you. In other words, what are your goals and how do you prioritize them?

In addition, it's important to begin the process of developing an internal schedule. Everyone, yourself included, works best in a given manner. You've most likely heard of so-called morning people and those who are referred to as night owls. Each individual person works best according to their own personal, flexible schedule. It is critical that you learn early on what works for you and what doesn't. Do not allow yourself to fall into the trap of believing that simply because a certain schedule works for someone else; it will work for you as well. That simply isn't true. Take the time to find out your own personal schedule and you'll quickly learn that it becomes much easier to handle both the tasks that are required of you and those that are important to you.

It's also important to begin understand how well you may already plan and how much improvement you may need in this area in order to begin managing your time efficiently. Presented below are several questions to help you make this self-assessment. Remember, it's important that you answer each question honestly based on your own feelings, rather than what you think the 'right' answer may be.

1. Do you make a to-do list?	Never	Seldom	Sometimes	Often	Always
2. Are you flexible with your plans?	Never	Seldom	Sometimes	Often	Always
3. How often do you accomplish what you plan?	Never	Seldom	Sometimes	Often	Always
4. Do you plan for things that are personally important to you?	Never	Seldom	Sometimes	Often	Always
5. Do you make plans in order to keep things in your life under control?	Never	Seldom	Sometimes	Often	Always
6. How often are your plans hindered by interruptions?	Never	Seldom	Sometimes	Often	Always

How to Score:

For questions 1-5, award yourself 1 point for each Never; 2 points for each Seldom, 3 points for each Sometimes, 4 points for each Often and 5 points for each Always. For question 6, award yourself 5 points for Never, 4 points for Seldom, 3 points for Sometimes, 2 points for Often and 1 point for Always.

Tally your points and check below to discover your current planning assessment.

6 – 10 The bad news is that you are not currently engaged in active planning. The good news is that it isn't too late to begin developing healthy new habits that can help you in efficiently managing your time.

11 – 15 While it appears that you currently engage in some type of planning system, there is most likely a need to use it more efficiently.

16 – 20 On the surface, the planning system you are currently utilizing appears to be working, but there is a need for improvement in order to help you better handle interruptions and prioritize your activities.

21 – 25 Congratulations! It would appear that you have a handle on how to plan and prioritize your activities. Remember to do a periodic check-up to ensure that your goals continue to be met.

26 – 30 At this point it's important to be careful that you make a determination between planning well and obsessive control. Allow the fact that you have your activities under control provide peace of mind and don't stress the small things.

Now that you have a basic understanding of where you may already be on the planning playing field, it's time to get started with the basics of successful time management. As with any other task, there are certain tasks that are considered to be basic elements, or steps, of efficient time management.

The first step is to set specific and definable goals for yourself. These goals should be both career-oriented and personal.

Once your goals have been set, it's time to create a calendar. You can either choose to follow the calendar year, or the fiscal year of the company or your business. Begin by drafting your calendar; making sure you have reflected any major events like public non-working holidays, payment due dates, project deadlines, and other important dates.

After your calendar has been drafted, you can begin to drill that schedule down some by creating a weekly schedule. This schedule will reflect all activities that you are responsible for on a weekly basis; including your appointments, company meetings, client presentations, etc.

The previous two activities were probably relatively easy, as they were simply a matter of recording facts which were already in evidence. The next part may be slightly more difficult and will require you to bring in certain personal elements. As we discussed, it's important for you to understand your own personal, flexible schedule. This will be very important as you begin to plan for specific time in order for you to work on each course and activity.

Finally; you will need to create a to-do list for each day. This list should ideally be created the night before so that there is no doubt about how the following day should take shape. If your day runs long, however; you may find that you need to create your to-do list before or during breakfast each day. This is fine; as long as it is done. Making a to-do list for the day gives you an idea of the things you need to do and how much time you must allot to each task.

Presented in Appendix A is an example of a master daily schedule. Certainly you can purchase such blank calendars in any number of office supply stores. Depending on your own schedule, and personal preferences; you may prefer to create your own on a word processing program. Remember, that you do not need to get too technical in the form of the schedule. It is the content that matters.

So, how much time do you need to spend on your scheduling and how do you prioritize your activities; especially when your schedule already appears to be overbooked? An easy solution would be to let your secretary handle your schedule, but who is the one who's actually going to attend all those meetings and events? It's always a good idea to personally keep track of your schedule to avoid spreading yourself too thin on all your engagements and activities. Balancing the numerous activities and tasks required of you is no walk in the park. However, it IS possible.

One of the most common mistakes of scheduling is ironically trying to plan too far ahead. This can be a serious temptation. Whenever possible, it is always best to plan for only what already exists and then to add to your schedule only as events and activities pop up and become known.

The first activities that should appear on your schedule are those concerning your work. Don't make the mistake of thinking that you don't need to schedule for this. By outlining the time you would be spending at the office, you can easily fill in the times in between for the different tasks you do in the course of the day. Activities like the weekly company meeting, brainstorming sessions, teleconferences, catching up on correspondence, etc. It is inevitable for appointments to be canceled and moved, make your schedule as flexible as possible. Also bear in mind that meetings can go on for hours, so try to give allowances in between tasks. If you feel that your whole week is all about work work work, schedule some much needed rest and recreation time during the weekend as a treat to yourself and some quality time spent with the family.

A schedule will only work if you utilize it. Simply committing a list of activities to paper will not suddenly create a situation in which you can manage your time better. Keep your schedule in a prominent location where you can see it daily and refer to several times throughout the day.

Scheduling often fails for a variety of reasons. Presented below is a list of tips to help you avoid the most common traps that could prevent you from becoming successful at time management.

1. Don't allow yourself to think that any of your time expendable. Get into the habit of thinking of your time as a precious commodity.
2. Even mundane, routine tasks that you find displeasing can be easier to handle when you find at least one thing enjoyable about it – even if it is only a necessary activity on the way to something else you would prefer to do.
3. Don't forget to plan ahead. Get in the habit of reviewing your monthly calendar to anticipate how you might be able to better schedule your activities and time.
4. Reward yourself for important tasks accomplished.
5. Don't make exceptions and don't skip around. Do first things first.
6. If you find yourself avoiding a task or activity, face it head on and get it over with.
7. Whenever possible, set deadlines
8. Don't allow pride to be your downfall. If you need help or advice, ask for it.
9. Work on having an optimistic attitude and to see the good in all things.
10. Always be on the look out for ways to expand

upon your successes.

11. Don't cry over spilled milk! Instead of regretting your failures, make a point to learn from your mistakes.
12. Don't put yourself in a position where you miss out on the important things in life. Remember that if it's important to you; it's important to find the time to do it.
13. Always be on the lookout for ways to free up your time.
14. Make a habit of periodically reviewing your habits in order to determine whether your time could be better enhanced by changing them.
15. Always carry a small notepad or calendar with you so that you can write down reminder notes.
16. On a monthly basis, take the time to review your lifetime goals. Don't forget to make a note of your progress and congratulate yourself.
17. At the end of each day, review the tasks you needed to accomplish and evaluate your progress. Make adjustments where necessary.

When designing your schedules, there are certain tasks that can make both the design and implementation process much easier. Take a look:

People frequently comment that they do not have the time to accomplish the goals and activities that interest them most because they are too caught up in the activities that are required of them. Remember, if it's important to you; you should take the time to plan for it. Begin by recording any special activities you need to do or want to do on a regular basis.

In order to avoid being caught unprepared for your

meetings and presentations, make it a habit to schedule a 30-minute prep time. This can be used for you to rehearse your spiel or review the agenda for the meeting. That way, you feel confident and prepared when you're in front presenting to your client or to the management. Run through your visual aides, like a PowerPoint Presentation, to familiarize yourself with the sequence of the slides. If you have handouts, make sure each set have the same number of pages.

Schedule an hour or so first thing in the morning to catch up on correspondence. By allotting ample time to focus on this, it saves you from taking time off from work by checking your e-mail every hour. If you're expecting a response within the day, check again after lunch after your break. Lastly, schedule another hour before the end of the work day for sending out e-mails for the next day.

Numerous studies indicate that regular exercise helps to reduce stress and tension; while helping you to feel better about yourself and what you can accomplish. Take time out of your busy schedule for exercise to keep yourself fit and healthy. Go to the gym for short 30-minute workout during your lunch hour or jog in your neighborhood before going to work.

Don't over plan. Be flexible in your scheduling and leave some blocks of time open for canceled meetings, and re-scheduled appointments, and unplanned excursions.

Finally, allow time to relax and unwind. While this is best reserved for the weekends. Look at it as a reward for all the hard work you've put in during the week and for sticking to your schedule.

Presented below are several examples of different schedules, to help you begin developing an idea of how to efficiently manage your time. Note that these schedules are based on weekly and long-term formats, such as term, four year and beyond. While there is no need to use these exact formats; do make a point to insure that you not only plan for the present but the future as well.

Creating a Master Weekly Schedule

This activity allows you to account for all fixed and regular activities that are anticipated to remain the same for most of the semester. Begin by entering the following information:

- Enter your work schedule.
- Enter other routine meetings and responsibilities.
- Enter routine mealtime, travel time, sleep, exercise, laundry, shopping, etc.
- Enter regular times for recreation (social hobbies, athletics, private time.)

After your Weekly Master schedule is complete, you can construct a regular weekly schedule. Some find it helpful to plan their activities in blocks of 50 minutes each. This gives you the opportunity to follow each block with a 10 minute break.

Refer to the Table 1.1 in Appendix B.

Creating an Annual Calendar

When planning your annual calendar, it's important to keep all items from your regular weekly schedule as well as add in any other events that you expect will occur during the year. These events might include annual holidays, special occasions and anniversaries. Other things to note down are deadlines, project commencements and targeted project end, accounting period, etc.

Refer to the Table 1.2 in Appendix B.

Creating a Five Year Calendar

A five-year plan is one of the cornerstones of long range planning. This is a basis on the direction your life will take.

When handling this type of schedule, be sure to include the following types of activities:

- All relevant career path your are taking or plan to take
- Trips and vacations
- Further studies
- Relocation

Refer to the Table 1.3 in Appendix B.

Creating a To-Do list

We'll go into a little more detail regarding to-do lists later, but for now we'll cover some of the basics. Creating a to-do list is an easy and simply way to transfer important items from any schedule to a manageable list that can be easily accessed any time and anywhere.

You may find that it works better for you to create your list the night before or to handle it that morning. Whichever method you prefer, begin by using a 3x5 card that can easily fit into your pocket. Refer to your weekly schedule and jot down activities that have priority for today.

As these activities are completed, you can cross them off. Any activities that are not completed should be carried over to the next day. Although, a word of caution on the latter; too much of this can get you into a serious time constraint. Aim for what you can realistically accomplish.

Chapter 2 Setting Goals and Priorities

As previously mentioned, when learning to manage your time it is important to not only commit the activities and tasks that are required of you to paper, but also to begin developing a statement of your long-range goals. The long-term and four year planning calendars are one way to begin doing this; however, in order to maximize the effectiveness of this type of planning it is imperative that you become explicit and specific in your goals statements.

In goal setting, you will do much more than simply state "This is what I want to do in _____ amount of time." You must also set shorter range goals that will help you to meet your long term goals as well as prioritize the specific steps necessary for you to accomplish those goals. While this may at first seem to be an easy enough task; it can become more difficult than you might imagine as you face the prospect of having to confront your own bad habits and the reality of completing tasks that you might otherwise desire to put off.

One of the most difficult aspects of drafting long term plans is in understanding where to begin and then how to drill them down to manageable tasks that can be accomplished in sequence over a period of time. Below is an example of a long term goal and the intermediate and short term goals that are related.

Long-Term Goal: Buy a house in the country

Intermediate Goals:

1. Invest in time deposit or stocks
2. Get promoted to a higher position or switch to another company that offers better opportunity for growth and has competitive compensation package.

Short-Term Goals (Present):

1. Network more.
2. Meet, and if possible, exceed targeted number of closed deals for the month/quarter/year.

Daily, Weekly, and Annual Scheduling

The key to successful time management is in not only planning your daily and weekly schedule, but also in insuring that you have developed a schedule for your obligations each year. This is extremely important because it will help you to keep your intermediate goals in mind and prevent you from exchanging one activity for another. By constantly being aware of tasks looming on your annual schedule, you will be more likely to stick your weekly and daily schedule in order to remain on track with your plans.

One way to handle planning your daily activities is to simply make a list of everything that you both want and need to accomplish throughout the day. By taking this a step further, you can then prioritize these activities. This type of schedule works very well for a daily planning tool; however, it can also be modified to cover other periods of time as well. For individuals who prefer not to be chained to an hour by hour schedule, this solution can be a satisfying compromise.

Priority can be handled in a number of ways; such as either numerically or alphabetically. For example 1= Highest Priority, 2= Moderate Priority, 3= Lowest Priority or likewise with an alphabetical system; A = Highest Priority, B = Moderate Priority, C = Lowest Priority.

Take a look at the sample schedule below:

Monday
1. Finish and double check documents for submission due on Wednesday (A)
2. Research for next project due next month (C)
3. Prepare for client meeting on Friday (B)
4. Compile relevant documents for the board meeting on Thursday (A)
5. Meet wife for dinner (B)
6. Approve and affix signatures for all correspondence, reports and documents for signing (B)
7. Buy gift for daughter's 8th birthday on Saturday (C)

This type of schedule allows for a great deal of flexibility; by allowing you to commit to a balanced schedule that allows for work responsibilities as well as personal desires.

Regardless of what system you elect to use in order to prioritize your tasks, it is essential that you commit the activities that you must accomplish on paper. You may either purchase a calendar or planner for such purpose or simply write them down on a notebook or note card that you can carry with you throughout the day.

If you are the type of person that needs more structure; you may need a schedule that allows for less flexibility. The hour by hour schedule mentioned and presented in the previous sections works very well for this purpose. The most important key to insuring that an hour by hour schedule is successful is being realistic in your scheduling. Make sure you schedule time for recreation and free time. Failure to do so can quickly lead to burn out and a complete abandonment of the system.

Balance

Every schedule, regardless of style or design, must have balance. Everyone, no matter what their personal desires and goals may happen to be, need a balanced life-style in order to be efficient, successful and happy.
When you fail to complete a balanced schedule for yourself, your very health will reflect it. Many succumb to health problems because of this very issue. Remember to pay attention to following important areas of your life in order to avoid this trap:

- Physical (exercise, nutrition, sleep)
- Intellectual (cultural, aesthetic)
- Social (intimate and social relationships)
- Career (career goal directed work)
- Emotional (expression of feelings, desires)
- Spiritual (quest for meaning)

You do not necessarily need to schedule activities for each and every one of these areas and certainly not for every day; however if you fail to take care of one of these areas in your life, you are definitely setting yourself up for trouble.

Procrastination, Distractions, and Other Problems

As previously mentioned, a big problem with the success of many time management and scheduling plans occurs when distractions intervene and many allow themselves to procrastinate to the point that not only are their short term goals compromised, but their intermediate and long term goals as well. For example, if you fail to prepare and finish your presentation for a client your company has been targeting to get for years, there's a big chance you will do poorly and lose the account. Worse yet, you just might not get that promotion you were aiming for.

To avoid these types of problems, take a look at the following tips:

1. Ask for help and cooperation from those around you. Allow your spouse, family members, co-workers and others know about your efforts to manage time.
2. Allow time to be spontaneous.
3. Be realistic in your planning approach and do not set yourself up to fail.
4. Make sure you jot down your schedules and priorities on paper.
5. Review your long-term and intermediate goals often. Keep a list where you will see it often.
6. Continually try to eliminate unnecessary tasks that are not related to your goals or to maintaining a balanced life style.
7. Take advantage of your natural cycles, schedule the most difficult activities when you are at your best.
8. Learn to say "No" to people, including spouses,

friends, children, and parents.

9. Reward yourself for effective time management.

Chapter 3 Strategies for Time Management

Developing skills that will help you to better manage your time is a path that will continue to evolve throughout most of your life. Like any other skill set, you need to spend time practicing these skills in order to hone them to peak efficiency.

While it is important to develop your own style for managing your time and work, consider how the following techniques might help you.

It is critical to take advantage of your own natural time management. You may have heard of the term biological rhythms. This term refers to the times of day when your energy levels are at their highest and when you can accomplish your most important work. If you are a morning person, don't put off important activities until late in the evening. Reserve your low energy periods of time for tasks that do not require much concentration, such as handling your laundry.

You can also create a situation in which you can more efficiently manage your tasks and activities by optimizing your work environment.

Give some thought to how you work best. Do you prefer to have music playing while you work or do you consider it to be a distraction? Take these things into consideration when designing your work environment.

Chapter 4 Facts and Myths

Unfortunately, many people never get started on the path to efficient time management because they buy into a number of myths that persuade them to believe that it simply won't work for them and isn't worth the time or effort. Conversely, individuals often get caught up in using time management techniques that have proven successful for others; but may be woefully inadequate for their own needs. When the methods fail, they are even more confused, stressed and discouraged than when they began. The most important thing to remember about any time management technique is that it must be geared towards the goals that are important to you and must include techniques for effective prioritizing.

Let's take a look at some of the most common myths that commonly lead to poor time management.

MYTH: Events outside my power control my life.

FACT: You always have at least some control over certain events in your life. Furthermore, you and only you have the responsibility for exerting that control. Make a point to learn what you can control and what you can't. Look ahead to the future to anticipate demands on your time that you can't control. This will help you to determine what you can do within a reasonable amount of time; regardless of external events.

MYTH: I need to be able to do everything everyone expects of me.

FACT: You simply can't be everything to everyone. The needs and demands of others may not be timed right in order for you to meet them or they simply be impossible for you to meet at this time. While important to others, they may not be a priority to you. By attempting to meet all the needs and demands of other people, you will create a situation in which you fall short of meeting the goals that are important to you. Focus first on the needs and desires that are important to you before you try to meet the expectations of others.

Chapter 5 Developing Priorities

Developing priorities is critical to any successful time management technique. Without priorities it can be difficult to get anything accomplished or focus on the most critical tasks.

To begin the process of developing your own personal set of priorities, ask yourself the following questions.

- What is the purpose of the job?
- What are the measures of success?
- What is exceptional performance?
- What kind of job is this?
- How do you achieve this?
- What are the priorities and deadlines?
- What resources are available?
- What costs are acceptable?
- How does this relate to other people?
- What is the broader picture within which you have to work?

Take a look at the following steps to help you begin assessing how to prioritize the tasks and activities you must accomplish.

Begin by developing an overview of everything that you want to accomplish. First, determine the time frame you'd like to work with. This may be on a long term basis such as a year, an intermediate basis such as a month or on a short term basis such as a week or a day.

Be sure to include not only your career but your personal goals as well; such as spending more time friends or family, dedicating some time to physical activity a specific number of times per week or even making time to watch the NBA finals live. Whatever your goals may happen to be for your specified time frame; write them on separate index cards.

Next, organize your goals according to their priority. Determine the urgency of each goal that you have set and then separate them into two stacks; one stack for those goals that you have determined to be urgent and another for those that you deem to be non-urgent. For example; preparing for your big presentation and watching the NBA Finals may be more urgent than other tasks because of deadlines that are attached to these goals.

Take the stack of urgent goals and further divide them into two categories: one representing items that are important and another representing items that are non-important. Do the same with the stack of non-urgent goals.

This type of method will help you to determine the priority of your goals and which are deemed to be important and urgent versus important but non-urgent. By utilizing a prioritizing method you can devote more time and energy to accomplishing the tasks that are important and urgent without wasting critical time on low priority tasks.

Regardless of what type of prioritizing system that you choose to use; it is critical that you begin to look ahead. Failure to look ahead and anticipate demands on your team can lead you to being caught unaware and forcing yourself to neglect other goals you intended to accomplish in order to cram for the upcoming goal.

To avoid this type of scenario devise a long range timetable for yourself. In your table, identify career goals and deadlines such as presentations and project completion. Remember annual staff reports both giving them for your staff and receiving them from your boss. Also include target dates for goals that are personal in nature. Determine whether there are any steps that you need to accomplish in order to complete these goals. For example, if you're making a study that would require you to travel out of state or out of the country, you need to schedule it ahead of time. Try to divide the larger activities into as many small chunks as possible. Then design a reasonable timeline in which you believe you can realistically accomplish these goals.

Many executives attempt to ignore certain activities in order to create more time for themselves. This almost never works and always catches up with you. There are certain daily activities that you must take care in order to keep your life orderly and on track. Failure to obtain enough sleep, for example; will always result in negative side effects. If you allow your laundry to pile up you will certainly realize that you have nothing appropriate to wear on the day of your big presentation in speech class. Skip enough meals and you'll find yourself in the emergency room. You get the point. Don't avoid these activities— plan for them.

Always allow room for flexibility. Some things are just inevitably going to occur that you have no control over and while you cannot plan for those exact circumstances you can leave enough room in your schedule to adjust your plans for unexpected events.

Chapter 6 Procrastination

One of the biggest creators of problems for almost everyone is procrastination. Sometimes you may not even be aware that the delays you are implementing are actually procrastination. To the naked eye, they can appear to be valid reasons for putting off your work. Take a look:

- "One more day won't make any difference; I'll just put that off until tomorrow."
- "It won't matter if I'm a few minutes late; no one else will be on time."
- "I work best under pressure."
- "I'll watch just 15 more minutes of TV."
- "I can't start on this presentation until I know just how I want the first paragraph to read."
- I can't write the rest of this report until I write the introduction

Beating procrastination is one of the best things you can do to change your time management habits. Procrastination can take on many forms, but in its essence it involves putting off tasks that you should be doing now. While you may have very good intentions of handling the task later; there is very little chance this will happen. If you do return to the task, there's a high likelihood that you will give it less than your best because you waited to the last minute.

Procrastination occurs for a number of different reasons. The most common are waiting for the right mood to strike or waiting for the right time.

If you find yourself frequently giving these reasons as an excuse for putting off tasks and activities then you need to examine your schedule activities. In all likelihood, you'll find the presence of one or more of the following factors:

- Lack of clear goals
- Underestimating the difficulty of the tasks
- Underestimating the time required to complete the tasks
- Unclear standards for the task outcomes
- Feeling as the tasks are imposed on you from outside
- Too ambiguous tasks

And there are also many connections with:
- Underdeveloped decision making skills
- Fear of failure or fear of success
- Perfectionism

Avoiding procrastination is as simple as developing good decision making skills and techniques. Decision making can appear to be a complex issue and skill on the surface. In reality it is nothing more than choosing one course of action from several possibilities. Look at it as multiple choice for life.

The difference between choosing among the multiple choice possibilities in the tests you used to take in school, and the possible alternatives for your weekly schedule, is that the possibilities on your exam may include options that are clearly wrong. Life is not all peaches and cream. Make your life as enjoyable as possible by choosing the alternatives that would give you a positive outcome.

You can begin developing good decision making skills by taking three steps. First, identify the purpose of your decision. What's the problem and why do you need to solve it? Next, gather the information you need to solve the problem and come up with possible solutions. After evaluating each option in terms of possible consequences, decide which alternative is best.

The only thing left to do is to put your decision into action and stick with it.

Chapter 7 Special Time Management Issues

Do you find yourself frequently commenting that you can't stick to a schedule because something always pops up, or interrupts or causes you to deviate from your intended plans?

This is actually a common complaint and none of us are immune to these types of issues. The difference between individuals who make a time management program work and those who fall victim to these issues, is learning to identify common time wasters and handle them appropriately.

Take a look below at the list of most common reasons for reducing effectiveness.

- Interruptions - telephone
- Interruptions - personal visitors
- Meetings
- Unclear communication
- Inadequate technical knowledge
- Unclear objectives and priorities
- Lack of planning
- Stress and fatigue
- Inability to say "No"
- Personal disorganization
- Tasks you should have delegated
- Procrastination and indecision
- Acting with incomplete information
- Dealing with team members
- Crisis management (fire fighting)

While these issues are common to most people; there are ways to handle them so that you can be more in control of the situation and reduce your stress in order to still accomplish your goals despite these time wasters.

Before we explore the ways to handle these issues, let's look at why they create such a problem.

Lack of priorities and objectives is perhaps one of the easiest ways to waste times. Without a clear map of where you want to go, you'll get nowhere.

Attempting to take on too much will only result in projects that are only partially completed and leave you with a feeling of failure.

Everyone has to deal with people who drop in at the last minute or try to impose their own problems on your already packed schedule. Learning how to deal with these type of people situations is one of the best ways you can get a handle on your schedule and learn to manage your time effectively.

Delegation is the key. Everyone needs to learn how to effectively delegate. Successful managers and leaders make it an art form. The problem is that many people dislike delegating because they are afraid that someone else won't do the task nearly as well as they would. While this may be true, this type of mindset will only keep you bogged down. Ask yourself if someone else could do the job at least as well as 80% as you would. If your answer is yes, you should delegate it.

Do you ever find that you waste precious minutes, even hours, looking for important items? While college living isn't conducive to wide open spaces, the more clutter you can eliminate the more effective you will be at handling all your tasks.

Procrastination is one of the biggest time thieves. Try to avoid putting off your tasks and get in the habit of making decisions instead of putting them off.

One simple word can help to eliminate a significant amount of you stress. No! Far too often people take on too much because they're too nice or shy to simply say "No!" Remember that there is nothing wrong with this word; in a sense, it can be savior of your sanity.

Below are some tips on how you can get a handle on these time wasters in order to better manage your time.

As soon as you possibly can do so, define your goals and objectives. This is one of the most common traits of the most successful people in the world.

The most important question you can always ask yourself is, "Right now; what is the most important way I can utilize my time?" This question will help you to focus on important tasks and avoid spending time on tasks that will get you nowhere.

Always have a plan. Regardless of your goals; you will be able to accomplish few of them without a plan. Make it a point to review your plans frequently and update them accordingly as changes occur. Balance the time spent planning against the time spent doing.

You can't put an end to all problems, but good time management will enable you to respond appropriately and be flexible enough to ensure that even problems won't completely derail your goals.

On your daily to do list, make sure that you have accounted for potential interruptions. Also, assign a deadline to each task and estimate how much time you anticipate each task will require. Then, stick to your plans. If you know that you frequently get derailed by certain interruptions; try to plan for them.

For many executives, the effort of trying maintain a healthy balance between their work and their home life; many times while also trying to manage a job is simply too much. Short of winning the lottery, there isn't much that can be done about whittling down the tasks that you are responsible for, but having a plan in place can help you to manage these tasks more efficiently.

Let's face it, most of your daily tasks can get quite mundane and routine after years of doing them. The good news about this is that you can easily develop a system that will help you to work smarter, not harder.

In regards to planning household work, there are a few different ways you can approach the tasks that need to be handled. The most common way to handle it, for most people, is to do it themselves. However, you need not take on every single task in your household if there are others around who can help to lighten the load.

In today's modern homes, the practice of each person taking care of their own responsibilities is growing increasingly popular. This would include tasks such as laundry, meals, cleaning, shopping, etc. While this may not be practical for everyone; it's definitely worth considering.

You can also delegate the household tasks that you are responsible for to other individuals. In order for this to work well, you need to take the following steps:

- Teach the person how to do the job, including any shortcuts that you may be aware of that can make the job go easier and faster.
- Have the best tools, supplies, and equipment for doing the job.
- Consider what household work a person already does.
- Never re-do a job (unless health and/or safety is threatened). If you do, you'll get the job back and in the end you'll ultimately be wasting more time than you're saving.
- Realize others may not meet your standards, but if you have truly given up the job, accept that your standards no longer apply. Generally speaking; if someone else can accomplish the job at least as well as 80% of the way you could handle it, then that's good enough.
- Never forget to say thank-you.

The final option would be to hire someone to handle the work for you. Unlike the time when you were still a college student living off on student loans, you are now making a considerable amount of money to let you pay for hired help. Options run from a live-in maid, cook and housekeeper, or a gardener to tend the yard work every weekend. If you think this still pretty much out of your budget, you still have other options. For example, what about asking a teenager in your neighborhood to drop by every two weeks to give the place a good once over? That won't be exorbitantly expensive and you'll both benefit.

If you are responsible for the preparation of any portion of your meals, there are also some tips you can implement that will help you to save time in this area as well. One of the best ways to do this is to implement a rotating menu system. You may choose to use either complete meals, including side dishes; on this menu or stick with hearty main dishes. Make a master shopping list for all the ingredients needed to prepare the meals on your master menu and keep it handy so that you can check off items as you run out of them. Consider either placing it on the fridge with a magnet or tucking it into a drawer next to the stove or pantry. Another option is to teach your teenager how to cook. That way, if you have an impromptu appointment and will be late in coming home, he can take over the cooking for you.

To avoid wasting time with numerous weekly shopping trips, plan for only one large shopping trip each month. You can save even more time by cooking meals in large quantities and freezing the leftovers to create meals that can be warmed up in just a matter of minutes.

Clothing and laundry can also be handled in such a way as to free up a little more of your time. If there are small children in your household, it may seem inconceivable to you but children over the age of 3 can actually put up their own laundry. You may need to reconcile yourself to the fact that it won't be done the way you would have done it, but it will be finished.

Further simplify laundry by using baskets and hampers that have been labeled or color coded for washing machine settings. Keep the laundry near your laundry facilities to keep from having to track it down. To speed up the process of putting away completed laundry, get in the habit of moving laundry from the dryer to baskets that have been labeled for specific member of the family so that they can easily and quickly locate their own stuff when it's time to put it away.

House cleaning can also tend to sneak up on you. Try setting aside either Friday night or Saturday morning as your day for taking care of these matters. Get everyone involved. Similar to laundry, set up a house rule that everyone over the age of 3 is responsible for picking up their own room.

Take the plunge and keep multiple sets of cleaning supplies in separate locations throughout the house so that no one has the excuse of not being able to locate the right cleaner in order to take care of a mess as it occurs.

The morning rush to get out the door can be an easy way to lose precious moments and create a stressful feeling that persists throughout the day. Eliminate this tendency by setting up one consistent area where everyone can place their briefcases, purses, backpacks, etc. the night before so they are can be easily located the next morning.

Meetings
Meetings are often times a necessary evil; regardless of where you happen to be in your life. When you were still in college, you have no doubt often got caught up in meetings for study groups and extra-curricular activities. In your professional career, the amount of meetings attended is almost literally double the number you faced in college, and you realize that you could often get more accomplished without them.

Since eliminating meetings altogether isn't an option for most people, instead try to get more out of them by using the following tips.

If you're responsible for running meetings, check out the following ideas:
1. Hold meetings only when trigger events occur. Contrary to popular opinion, it's really not necessary to hold regular meetings when there is absolutely no reason to do so.

2. Use the Agenda Effectively
The agenda of the meeting shows the aim of the meeting, and points of discussion in priority order - effectively it is a To Do List for the meeting. The agenda can help you to stop wanderers from drifting away from the subject at hand and ensure that everyone is fully prepared.

3. Setting the time of the meeting
Keep in mind that the time when you schedule your meeting can best be determined by the habits of those who attend the meeting. For example; if you notice that the attendees frequently drone on and on; set the meeting for a time of day when everyone is anxious to either return home or get back to another activity.

Also keep in mind that you better utilize your meetings by only bringing in the number of people that are necessary to conduct a successful meeting. Inviting additional people will only lead to increased discussion and consequently, wasted time.

Even if you are not responsible for running meetings, you

can still exercise some control over making sure that you maximize the experience. Check out the following tips:

- Always be on time, and present only if you are needed
- Be well prepared and briefed on your contribution
- Remain attentive to the discussion so that your contribution does not repeat someone else's
- Be involved in the discussion

Using Waiting Time

It happens to be the best of us. As much as we try to avoid it and as much as we plan, life is going to involve a certain amount of waiting. For most people, this amount of time is often viewed as wasted time. It doesn't have to be wasted time; however, if you learn how to use it effectively.

- Always confirm your appointment the day before.
- Don't arrive more than 5 minutes early.
- Always have something with you to work on during unavoidable delays.

Do you find that your plans are often interrupted by a call from your wife? Instead of waiting for her to call you when you're in the middle of concentrating on your presentation piece, plan for this and pick up the phone and call her instead.

To make sure that you don't spend more time than you can afford on phone calls, set a specific time limit for the amount of time you can spend on the phone call. Also, try developing notes of what you intend to say or find out during your call and then stick to them. Keep yourself from feeling deprived of much needed phone time with your relatives and friends, allot a time during the weekend or the day when your schedule is mostly free. That way, you get your necessary work done and still have the chance for a once-a-week catching up with your loved ones.

Also; never give in to the pressure to be placed on hold. Instead, ask for a time when you can call back or leave your name and telephone number for them to return your call. The same applies when an individual is not able to take your call.

If you're on a deadline and can only spend a certain amount of time on the phone; let the person on the other end of the line know that up front. Better yet, have your secretary screen your calls. Only allow people involved in the project or presentation that you're currently focusing on to interrupt you.

Avoid the scramble of trying to find haphazardly written messages by keeping a pen and pad by the telephone.

Spending time searching for items you need can take away from a significant portion of your schedule. Learn to combat this by taking time to tidy as you go along. Items that are not relevant should be discarded. Break the habit of thinking "What if…" Try to keep as many items as possible off the top of your desk. Set specific places or desk drawers for your items. The top of the desk can be adorned with reference books, a pen holder, a note pad and or a couple of pictures. If your desk has built in drawers, assign one exclusively for pens, pencils, highlighters, permanent markers, calculator, paper clips, stapler, etc. The other drawer can hold clean bond paper.

Try to maintain this order so you always know where your things are.

To effectively deal with drop in visitors, try the following suggestions:

As soon as the visitor arrives, establish why they've come to see you. Some people can waste an hour or more of your time before they ever get around to explaining the real reason why they dropped by. Few people stop by just to chat.

When you answer the door, remain standing. This almost forces the other person to remain standing and prevents them from 'settling' in.

Similar to the tip for dealing with phone calls; explain to the visitor that you only have a specific amount of time to dedicate to this conversation. Avoid engaging in small talk.

Chapter 8 Review: Developing Time Management Skills

As previously mentioned throughout this book, there are numerous techniques and tools that you can utilize to take control of the time allotted to you for completed necessary and important tasks. Below we will review the most pertinent of these techniques. This will help you to develop a clear idea of how you can efficiently manage your time.

Estimating the Cost of your Time

Many people fail to realize how much inefficiently handling their time can actually cost them. They assume that if they are getting paid for their time, their time is their own. They fail to calculate the real cost of wasting time.

By estimating the cost of your time, you can assess whether you are spending your time profitably and gauge whether you need to make necessary changes.

In the corporate world, this is done by calculating how much your time costs each year in terms of salary, payroll taxes and even the cost for the office space where you work. Other expenses such as equipment, various expenses and administrative support are also tallied in.

The next step is to figure the amount of money you think you should earn from your activity.

To this figure add a 'guesstimate' of the amount of profit you should generate by your activity. Begin by estimating the amount of time you spend on your activities per year. For example; if you spend roughly 8 hours per day on work over 300 days each year that equates to 2,400 hours per year.

Now, it's time to calculate an hourly rate. This will tell you how much your time is worth. Are your surprised at the amount?

Be sure to keep this amount in mind when you are faced with having to make a decision regarding whether to tackle a task or not. Based on the expected yield of task, do you think you would be spending your time wisely or wasting it?

Creating To Do Lists

A to-do list is considered one of the best ways to quickly and easily manage your time. Less bulky than a long-range calendar, a to do list gives you the opportunity to consolidate all the tasks you must accomplish in one location. In order to be effective; however a to do list must also be prioritized, with the tasks listed in order of importance so that you can take care of them first.

Individuals who feel that they have too much to do or feel as though they are frequently caught off guard, can eliminate much of their stress by implementing a to do list.

Preparing a to do list is not at all difficult. It involves simply writing down the activities and task that you must accomplish. When you run across complex or large tasks, simplify them by breaking them down into manageable chunks.

After this is accomplished, you can then begin to prioritize the tasks from those that you consider to be very important to those that are unimportant at this time. You may use either a numerical or alphabetical system in order to denote importance.

Once this is done, review your list to insure that you have a proper balance. If you find that too many tasks appear to have a high priority you may need to move less important tasks to a lower priority.

Scheduling Projects

Deadlines are often the impetus that either drive people to get busy or pour more stress on top of an already simmering fire. If you find that you frequently leave your work until the last minute with a final panic towards the end and that your final product has numerous errors as a result, you can most likely benefit from learning how to better schedule projects.

The first step you should take with any project is to make sure that you understand what is to be produced and then begin breaking the project down into smaller sections. Next, estimate the amount of time that will be required for each task and allow plenty of time to review your progress. This type of monitoring system will allow you to quickly respond to problems as they occur rather than realizing at the last minute that you have failed to allow enough time to complete the project.

Since there are no absolutes to any situation in life, there will always occur at least one situation in which you run across an impossible deadline. There are several ways in which you can handle such a situation. One way, ironically the most popular among those inexperienced in efficient time management, is to completely avoid the situation and hope that it will go away on its own. This rarely happens, however.

Realistically, you can either choose to have the deadline extended, obtain additional resources, ask to have the final product defined to something you can actually accomplish or let the person in charge of the project know early on that you are experiencing difficulties.

Understanding Where your Time Goes

There is an old cliché that says time flies when you're having fun. The same can also be true when you're pressed to the wall for a deadline. If you find that you frequently encounter a pressing deadline with no idea where the allotted time for the project went, it's a good idea to begin keeping track of how you use your time.

This can be done by using a weekly schedule to keep track of how use each hour of your waking day. This may seem a little mundane at first, but the result of such a personal assessment can be both enlightening and surprising.

After you have conducted such an assessment, it's time to learn from the research you have gathered. This is where putting the information you learn into use can begin to truly make a difference in how you manage your time. For example; if you discovered through your personal assessment that you typically sleep eight hours each night, then you will also learn this gives you 112 hours per week to accomplish all your tasks and activities.

Now, this sounds like a lot of time but you must keep in mind that everything must be crammed into those 112 hours including eating, doing your laundry, handling your personal hygiene, working, spending time with family and friends and even time unwinding in front of the TV. Absolutely everything must be accounted for in your schedule.

The sample schedule in the next page will help you to learn how to best use this tool.

Activities	Hours per Day	Total Number of Days	Total Hours per Week
On average; how many hours do you sleep during a 24 hour time period? Be sure to include your average nightly sleep as well as naps.			
On average; how many hours per day do you require for grooming? On average; how many hours per day do you spend on meals? Don't forget to include any time required to prepare the food and clean-up afterwards.			
How much time do you spend each day traveling to and from work? Don't forget to add in the amount of time it takes to find a parking spot and walk to your office.			

How many hours per day do you spend on errands such as shopping, picking up dry cleaning, fueling your car, etc?			
How many hours per day do you spend on activities such as hobby clubs, church, etc?			
How many hours per day do you spend at work?			
How many hours per day do you spend entertaining guests for work?			
How many hours per day do you spend on entertainment such as visiting with friends, watching tv, going out, etc?			

Remember that in order for this type of assessment to truly work, you must be completely honest with yourself. By analyzing this type of weekly schedule you can begin to schedule your activities more efficiently and even begin to plan ahead to avoid last minute cramming. The key to making this work is to take the time to continually update your schedule. If necessary, make a point to pull an hour out of your schedule when necessary to enter pertinent data such as due dates for projects, presentations, reports, etc.

When entering the due dates, don't forget to allow plenty of time to work on the assignments and build in extra time for unforeseen events.

When scheduling your activities make sure you don't fall into the trap of being overbooked. When you schedule too much, you put yourself at risk for impending disaster when events beyond your control occur. For example, if you wait until the last minute to type your quarterly report because you've had several other activities that have required attention, you could create serious trouble for yourself when your computer crashes.

The general rule of thumb here is to only plan for about 50% of your time. This may not sound like a lot, but when you stop and thing about the number of interruptions and emergencies that can sneak up and destroy your well laid plans, you'll be glad you built flexibility into your schedule.

Chapter 9 Some Final Tips

Before you start on any project, it is important to make sure that you first understand the exact nature and requirements of the assignment or project. If you have any questions, ask them before you begin working instead of putting them off until later.

If you happen to be working on the assignment in a group setting, insure that everyone in the group fully understands the task at hand.

Start your scheduling of the assignment by listing all tasks you must accomplish to complete the project.

Only after you have listed the task, should you begin to prioritize them. Mark them in order of importance, writing a new list if necessary. Make sure you allot a reasonable amount of time to complete the tasks.

As necessary, delegate responsibilities. This is especially true when working in a group. Don't try to take it all on yourself. Divide up tasks equally and fairly.

After you have finished the planning phase, it's time to get started. When you have finished each individual task, be sure to cross it off your to-do list. Don't allow yourself to become distracted by other activities or tasks until you have completed the ones at hand.

In any environment, it can be very tempting to try to work with co-workers you consider as friends. This should only be done if you can do it effectively. If you find yourself getting up caught in chatter about items that are unrelated to your assignment, it's time to move to a private work location.

Research time can be an easy way to waste significant blocks of time. Avoid this by knowing what you are looking for. When doing research, avoid wasting time by knowing exactly what you are trying to find.

Avoid procrastination by following these tips:

- Don't procrastinate in getting started. Just do it.
- Don't be a perfectionist.
- If you find yourself putting off a task because it's boring, just go ahead and get it done so you don't have to deal with it any longer.

- Don't put things off until the last minute.

Planning for Good Health

Not taking care of your health can have sneaky consequences in terms of destroying your plans. Get started on the right path by having a good breakfast each and every morning. If you have a tendency to start running down by mid-morning, pack a healthy snack to revive your energy. Avoid large lunches as this seems to create digestion problems with can lead to lower energy levels in the afternoon.

Do take time to rest. Plan for occasional ten or fifteen minute breaks in order to restore your thought processes and energy.

Don't allow yourself to become a victim of burn out by committing to more things than you can reasonably or realistically accomplish. Learn to say no and mean it.

If you have a tendency to be a perfectionist, learn to curb those tendencies or suffer the consequences. Perfectionists tend to be the worst at effective time management, because good is never quite good enough. Avoid putting unneeded effort into a project.

Beyond completely doing away with everything in order to get the most important tasks accomplished, learn to compromise by altering your life in more effective patterns. Sometimes all you may need to do is simply re-prioritize in order to get the important tasks accomplished. Be willing to commit to a regular review of your schedule in order to determine whether you may need to reconsider the amount of time you spend on certain activities.

Appendix A

	Mon	Tue	Wed	Thu	Fri	Sat	Sun
7-8	Dress & Breakfast	Dress & Breakfast	Dress & Breakfast	Dress & Breakfast	Dress & Breakfast		
8-9	Drive to Work	Drive to Work	Drive to Work	Drive to Work	Drive to Work		Golf
9-10	Correspondence	Correspondence	Correspondence	Correspondence	Correspondence		
10-11	Company Meeting			Board Meeting			
11-12		Lunch Meeting	Lunch Meeting			Lunch with the Family	Lunch with the Family
12-1	Lunch			Lunch	Lunch		
1-2							
2-3							
3-4							
4-5	Correspondence	Correspondence	Correspondence	Correspondence	Correspondence	Time with Kids	Time with Kids
5-6							
6-7	Dinner	Dinner	Dinner	Dinner	Dinner		
7-8							
8-9							
9-10							
11-12							

Appendix B

Table 1.1

Weekly Schedule	Monday	Tuesday	Wednesday	Thursday	Friday	Saturday	Sunday
7-8							
8-9							
9-10							
10-11							
11-12							
12-1							
1-2							

2-3						
3-4						
4-5						
5-6						
6-7						
7-8						
8-9						

Table 1.2

Long Term Planner
__/__/__ to __/__/__

Week of	Monday	Tuesday	Wednesday	Thursday	Friday	Saturday	Sunday
~							
~							
~							
~							
~							
~							

Table 1.3

Five-year Planning

	Fall	Winter	Spring	Summer
1st Year				
2nd Year				
3rd Year				
4th Year				
5th Year				

Appendix C

Included in this appendix you will find more forms and tools that can help you to become better organized and more efficiently manage your time.

ITINERARY

Name:	Date:
Location:	

CALL	ITEM	RESULT	RESCHEDULE
Name: Address:			
Name: Address:			
Name: Address:			
Name: Address:			
Name: Address:			
Name: Address:			
Name: Address:			

NOTES

Time Log
Name: _____
Date: _____

Start Time	Activity	Priority	Duration

To do list

Date	Priority	Activity	Start Date	Due Date
	_1 _2 _3			
	_1 _2 _3			
	_1 _2 _3			
	_1 _2 _3			
	_1 _2 _3			
	_1 _2 _3			

Important Date Sheet

Project	Client	Team Members	Reports Due	Presentations

Long-Term Goal:

1.

2.

3.

Intermediate Goals:

1.

2.

3.

4.

Short-Term Goals (Present):

1.

2.

3.

4.

5.

Activities	Hours per Day	Total Number of Days	Total Hours per Week
On average; how many hours do you sleep during a 24 hour time period? Be sure to include your average nightly sleep as well as naps.			
On average; how many hours per day do you require for grooming? On average; how many hours per day do you spend on meals? Don't forget to include any time required to prepare the food and clean-up afterwards.			
How much time do you spend each day traveling to and from work? Don't forget to add in the amount of time it takes to find a parking spot and walk to your office.			

How many hours per day do you spend on errands such as shopping, picking up dry cleaning, fueling your car, etc?			
How many hours per day do you spend on activities such as hobby clubs, church, etc?			
How many hours per day do you spend at work?			
How many hours per day do you spend entertaining guests for work?			
How many hours per day do you spend on entertainment such as visiting with friends, watching tv, going out, etc?			

Project Plan

Project	Particulars	Reminders	Due Date

Daily Activity Guide

Monday	Tuesday	Wednesday	Thursday	Friday	Saturday	Sunday

To-do List

Date: _____

Done	Task

Note:

_____

_____

_____

_____

www.ingramcontent.com/pod-product-compliance
Lightning Source LLC
Chambersburg PA
CBHW072044190526
45165CB00018B/1433